LIFE CYCLE OF A
HONEYBEE

by Noah Leatherland

Minneapolis, Minnesota

Credits

All images are courtesy of Shutterstock.com, unless otherwise specified. With thanks to Getty Images, Thinkstock Photo, and iStockphoto. Cover – irin-k. Recurring images – Blue Flourishes, Konde Hipe, uiliaaa, YummyBuum, tanyaya, Terdpong, WinWin artlab. 2 – Bk87, Kuttelvaserova Stuchelova. 4–5 – Dernkadel, Tomsickova Tatyana, Oksana Kuzmina, Andrei Shumskiy, Max Topchii, Ground Picture, Inside Creative House. 6–7 – Daniel Prudek, Hakim Graphy, weter78. 8–9 – Bk87, lkordela, Aleksandr Rybalko. 10–11 – Kuttelvaserova Stuchelova. 12–13 – Ihor Hvozdetskyi, bamgraphy. 14–15 – bamgraph* slowmotiongli. 16–17 – Irisha_S, Juice Flair. 18–19 – MakroBetz, Tyler Olson. 20–21 – Alexander Wallstrom, Hekla. 22–23 – Ihor Hvozdetskyi, Dredger, bamgraphy, Daniel Prudek, yod 67.

Bearport Publishing Company Product Development Team

Publisher: Jen Jenson; Director of Product Development: Spencer Brinker; Managing Editor: Allison Juda; Editor: Cole Nelson; Associate Editor: Naomi Reich; Associate Editor: Tiana Tran; Designer: Kim Jones; Designer: Kayla Eggert; Designer: Steve Scheluchin; Production Specialist: Owen Hamlin

Library of Congress Cataloging-in-Publication Data is available at www.loc.gov or upon request from the publisher.

ISBN: 979-8-89577-014-6 (hardcover)
ISBN: 979-8-89577-445-8 (paperback)
ISBN: 979-8-89577-131-0 (ebook)

© 2026 BookLife Publishing
This edition is published by arrangement with BookLife Publishing.

North American adaptations © 2026 Bearport Publishing Company. All rights reserved. No part of this publication may be reproduced in whole or in part, stored in any retrieval system, or transmitted in any form or by any means, electronic, mechanical, photocopying, recording, or otherwise, without written permission from the publisher. Bearport Publishing is a division of FlutterBee Education Group.

For more information, write to Bearport Publishing, 5357 Penn Avenue South, Minneapolis, MN 55419.

Contents

What Is a Life Cycle?. 4

Honeybees on the Farm. 6

Busy Workers 8

The Queen and Drones 10

Laying Eggs 12

All Grown Up 14

Sweet Honey 16

Spreading Swarms 18

The End of Life. 20

Life Cycle of a Honeybee. . . .22

Glossary 24

Index. 24

WHAT IS A LIFE CYCLE?

All living things go through different stages of life. We come into the world and grow over time. Eventually, we die. This is the life cycle.

As humans, we start life as babies. We grow into toddlers and children. Then, we become teenagers. Finally, we are adults and get even older. We may have babies of our own, and then the cycle begins again.

HONEYBEES ON THE FARM

Animals on the farm go through life cycles, too. Some farms have honeybees. Farmers raise these **insects** for the honey they make.

Bee farmers are often called beekeepers.

HONEYCOMB

WOODEN FRAME

Most farms have only a few hives, while larger farms may have more than 100.

A group of honeybees that lives together is called a colony. Farmers make hives for their colonies to live in. Inside the hives are wooden frames where the bees build honeycomb.

BUSY WORKER

A colony has three different types of bees. Most bees in a colony are **females** called worker bees. They do many jobs, including building the honeycomb. Worker bees make the cells with a special wax from their bodies.

A WORKER BEE

A CELL

Worker bees also collect **nectar** from flowers and turn it into honey. Then, they store the sweet substance in some of the honeycomb cells. This becomes food for the colony.

THE QUEEN AND DRONES

The queen bee is the most important type of bee. She keeps the colony working together. She also lays all the eggs. There is only one queen in a hive at a time.

THE QUEEN BEE WITH A MARK

Beekeepers sometimes mark the queen with a little paint so they can easily find her.

A DRONE BEE

The last kind of bees in a hive are drones. These **males** do not do any work in the hive. Their only job is to **mate** with the queen bee.

LAYING EGGS

The queen lays eggs into separate honeycomb cells. Some of the eggs are **fertilized**. Most of them will become workers. One may be a new queen. The unfertilized eggs will become drones.

AN EGG

A queen can lay more than 2,000 eggs a day.

A LARVA

Royal jelly is made by the youngest worker bees.

After three days, bee larvae (LAR-vee) **hatch** from the eggs. For the first few days, worker bees feed these babies royal jelly. This substance gives the larvae the **nutrients** they need to grow.

ALL GROWN UP

When a larva is big enough, a worker bee uses wax to seal the baby bee into its cell. Inside, the larva spins a **cocoon** around itself and changes into a pupa (PYOO-puh).

A PUPA

Bees grow eyes, legs, and wings at the pupa stage.

More than a week later, the bee is an adult. It chews through the wax covering its cell. Then, the bee joins the rest of the colony and starts doing its job.

SWEET HONEY

Often, worker bees make more honey than the colony needs. Beekeepers take this extra honey to sell and to eat. They wear special gear to keep from getting stung as they work.

Beekeepers must get honey without hurting the bees. Sometimes, they use smokers to send smoke into their hives. This calms the bees so the keepers can carefully remove the frames.

SPREADING SWARMS

If a colony becomes too big for its hive, worker bees raise a new queen. The old queen then leaves to start a new colony. She takes thousands of bees with her. This traveling group of bees is called a swarm.

Beekeepers want swarms to stay on their farms. So, they build more hives close by. Sometimes, they use bait, such as specially scented sprays, to guide swarms to the new hives.

THE END OF LIFE

Most honeybees do not live for very long. Worker bees may live up to six months, while drones live for only about eight weeks. Queen honeybees can live as long as five years.

Farmers sometimes build fences around hives to keep birds out.

Some honeybees die earlier than usual because of **predators**. Other insects, birds, and bears eat bees and may damage their hives. Beekeepers have to be careful to keep the hives safe.

LIFE CYCLE OF A HONEYBEE

A honeybee begins its life as an egg. A larva hatches and grows. Then, it spins a cocoon and turns into a pupa. Soon, it becomes an adult.

During its life, a honeybee helps make or care for new eggs in the hive. Eventually, the bee will die, but the eggs will hatch and become even more honeybees. This keeps the life cycle going!

Glossary

cocoon a covering that larvae make to stay safe as they change to pupae

females worker or queen honeybees, with the queen capable of laying eggs

fertilized made able to grow into a female bee

hatch to break out of an egg

insects animals with six legs and three main body parts

males bees whose job is to mate with the queen

mate to come together to produce young

nectar a sweet liquid made by plants

nutrients substances plants and animals need to grow and stay healthy

predators animals that hunt and eat other animals

Index

beekeepers 6, 10, 16-17, 19
cocoons 14, 22
drones 11-12, 20
eggs 10, 12-13, 22-23

honey 6, 9, 16-17
larvae 13-14, 22
predators 21
pupa 14, 22

queens 10-12, 18, 20
swarms 18-19
workers 8-9, 12-14, 16, 18, 20